First World War
and Army of Occupation
War Diary
France, Belgium and Germany

46 DIVISION
Divisional Troops
Royal Army Veterinary Corps
1/1 North Midland Veterinary Section
6 April 1915 - 28 February 1916

WO95/2681/4

The Naval & Military Press Ltd
www.nmarchive.com
Published in association with The National Archives

Published by

The Naval & Military Press Ltd

Unit 10 Ridgewood Industrial Park,

Uckfield, East Sussex,

TN22 5QE England

Tel: +44 (0) 1825 749494

www.naval-military-press.com

www.nmarchive.com

This diary has been reprinted in facsimile from the original. Any imperfections are inevitably reproduced and the quality may fall short of modern type and cartographic standards.

© Crown Copyright
Images reproduced by permission of The National Archives, London, England, 2015.

Contents

Document type	Place/Title	Date From	Date To
Heading	46th Division Divl Troops 1-1st Nth Mid'D Vety Section Mar 1915-Feb 1919		
War Diary	Barlin.	01/07/1917	28/07/1917
War Diary		01/02/1916	28/02/1916
War Diary		01/08/1915	20/09/1915
War Diary		01/03/1916	28/03/1916
War Diary	Noeux-Les-Mines	01/05/1917	08/05/1917
War Diary	Barlin	09/05/1917	30/05/1917
War Diary		01/10/1915	08/10/1915
War Diary		01/07/1915	29/07/1915
War Diary	In Field	02/12/1918	31/12/1918
War Diary	Fontes.	01/04/1917	10/04/1917
War Diary	Busnes	13/04/1917	17/04/1917
War Diary	Noeux-Les-Mines.	23/04/1917	27/04/1917
War Diary		01/12/1915	25/12/1915
War Diary	Larbret	01/09/1916	28/09/1916
War Diary		27/09/1916	27/09/1916
War Diary	In Field	22/10/1918	31/10/1918
War Diary		01/01/1916	27/01/1916
War Diary		01/06/1915	26/06/1915
War Diary		06/04/1915	19/04/1915
War Diary	Grincourt	01/01/1917	26/01/1917
War Diary		01/11/1915	24/11/1915
War Diary	In Field	01/10/1918	21/10/1918
War Diary	Mingoval	04/04/1916	29/04/1916
War Diary	Drouvin	01/09/1916	29/09/1916
War Diary		01/01/1916	27/01/1916
War Diary	In Field	24/01/1919	28/02/1919
War Diary	In Field	01/11/1918	19/11/1918
War Diary		01/05/1915	15/05/1915
War Diary	In The Field	12/01/1917	31/01/1917
War Diary	Grincourt	01/03/1917	28/03/1917
War Diary	Mezerolles	29/03/1917	29/03/1917
War Diary	Monchel	30/03/1917	30/03/1917
War Diary	Anvin	31/03/1917	31/03/1917
War Diary	Field	02/01/1919	23/01/1919
War Diary	Larbret	01/10/1916	30/10/1916
War Diary	Occoches	31/10/1916	31/10/1916
War Diary	In Field	03/02/1919	17/02/1919
War Diary	In Field	04/09/1918	30/09/1918
War Diary	Barlin	17/06/1917	29/06/1917
War Diary	In Field	20/11/1918	29/11/1918
War Diary		01/10/1917	31/10/1917
War Diary	Drouvin	01/08/1917	29/08/1917
War Diary		04/02/1918	26/02/1918
War Diary	In Field	01/05/1918	31/08/1918
War Diary		01/01/1918	29/01/1918
War Diary	Le Marais Sec.	02/12/1916	02/12/1916
War Diary	Doollens	02/12/1916	06/12/1916
War Diary	Grincourt	08/12/1916	28/12/1916

War Diary	Grincourt	29/06/1916	04/07/1916
War Diary	Soncamp O.35.a.8.6. Sheet 51.C.	08/07/1916	30/07/1916
War Diary	Grincourt	01/06/1916	03/06/1916
War Diary	Grincourt	02/06/1916	28/06/1916
War Diary		01/03/1918	31/03/1918
War Diary	Grincourt	01/02/1917	27/02/1917
Miscellaneous	Occoches	01/11/1916	01/11/1916
War Diary	St Riquier.	02/11/1916	30/11/1916
War Diary	In Field	03/11/1917	27/11/1917
War Diary	Bethune	01/12/1917	31/12/1917
War Diary	Barlin	01/06/1917	15/06/1917
War Diary	In Field	02/07/1918	31/07/1918
War Diary	In Field	01/06/1918	29/06/1918
War Diary	Soncamp Farm O35a.8.6. Sheet 51C.	01/08/1916	28/08/1916
War Diary	Roellecourt	01/05/1916	09/05/1916
War Diary	Grincourt	10/05/1916	28/05/1916
War Diary		28/07/1917	28/07/1917
War Diary		26/07/1917	26/07/1917
War Diary		01/02/1916	28/02/1916
Heading	WO95/2681/4		
Heading	1/1 N.M. Mob. Veb. Sec. (46th Div) March 1915-Dec 1915 Vol I		
Miscellaneous	To D.A.D.V.S. 46th Divsn.	04/12/1917	04/12/1917
Miscellaneous	1/1 NM Mob Vety Sec Vol III		
Miscellaneous	1/1 NM Mob Vety Sec Vol II		

46TH DIVISION
DIVL TROOPS

1-1ST NTH MID'D VETY SECTION

MAR 1915-FEB 1919

WAR DIARY
or
INTELLIGENCE SUMMARY

Army Form C. 2118.

Vol / 9

Place	Date	Hour	Summary of Events and Information	Remarks and references to Appendices
Barlin	1/7/17		Capt. J. Foam took over command of M.M.M. M.V. KtG Sec.	
			Reinforcement received SE 3097 Pte Roper E.W.	
	2/7/17		Evacuated - sick - home by barge	
			D. Day admitted to Royal Herbert Hospital LONDON.	
	3/7/17		Opr Advanced Post L/I/G.O. 3 men at Bully Grenay	
			Evacuated 18 horses (contagious cases) by train Handed 1 man & 3 Canadian and 6 by barge	
	4/7/17		M.V.S. moved to Bergues at 9 AM. arrived 11:30 AM. Marching in state 1 Off. 25 OR.	
	6/7/17		M.V.S. moved to Bergues - Sgt Sid promoted to rank of R.A. Staff Sgt. to complete establishment as per	
			T.T. 02476 Local Corps Order 66	
	3/7/17		Sgt Sid promoted to rank of R.A. Staff Sgt from 8/7/17 to 6/8/17	
	7/7/17		Pte Cox leave 6 England from 8/7/17 to 6/8/17	
	8/7/17		D. Day returned	
	9/7/17		Evacuated 10 horses (7 mange) from Bruay.	
	10/7/17		Sgt Peak arrived.	
			Sgt Peak promoted to R.A Staff Sgt as from 3/7/17 R.6.0.68	
	11/7/17		2014 Sgt Peak promoted to R.A Staff Sgt as from 3/7/17 R.6.0.68	
	12/7/17		T.T. 02471 Pte Hollis evacuated	
	13/7/17		M.V.S. to replace Staff Sgt Peak	
	15/7/17		Sgt Walker joined M.V.S. to replace Staff Sgt Peak returned to 22 Vty Hospital. Base Time	
	19/7/17		1142114 Sgt Walker	
	20/7/17		Evacuated 11 horses	
	21/7/17		3/6294 Pte Roper Leave 23/7/17 to 3/8/17	
	22/7/17		Pte Roper leave 23/7/17 to 3/8/17	
	23/7/17		.487/17	
	24/7/17		Pte Chile leave 24/7/17 Marching in state 1 Off 26 OR. Takes over 8 mange cases.	
	05/7/17		M.V.S. moved to Droven Pte Prince went on leave from 26/7/17	
	28/7/17		Inmates handed to 6 M.V.S. promoted to rank of R.A. corporal from 24/7/17	
			02436 Pte Poe	John Facer Capt. M.V.S. T.F.

Army Form C. 2118.

Army Form C. 2118.

WAR DIARY
or
INTELLIGENCE SUMMARY
(Erase heading not required.)

N°1 N.Z.M. Mob. Vety Section

Hour, Date, Place	Summary of Events and Information	Remarks and references to Appendices
Feb 1. 1916.	H⁄qrs N.Z.M. Mobile Vety Section billeted at VILLERS- COO-AULT. C.H.	
Feb 12. 1916.	Cpll H. Larkett promoted to rank of Sergeant (Temp) and attached to 139th Inf. Bgde. C.H. Pte H. M°Carthy promoted to rank of Corporal. C.H. During the foregoing period sick animals were evacuated by road to No 2 B.V.H, and the motor ambulance belonging to that Hospital was found invaluable for the more serious cases. C.H.	
Feb 20 1916	Marched to RIBEAUCOURT. C.H.	
Feb 28 1916	Marched to FIENVILLERS. C.H.	
	C. Hartley Capt AVC T. H⁄qrs N.Z.M Mob Vety Section	

Army Form C. 2118.

WAR DIARY
or
INTELLIGENCE SUMMARY. 1/1st Nth. Mid. Mob. Vety Section

(Erase heading not required.)

Instructions regarding War Diaries and Intelligence Summaries are contained in F. S. Regs., Part II. and the Staff Manual respectively. Title pages will be prepared in manuscript.

Hour, Date, Place	Summary of Events and Information	Remarks and references to Appendices
Aug 1. 1915.	Nth. Mid. Mobile Veterinary Section billeted at L. 15. d. 8. 1. on Map Sheet 27. C.H.	
Aug 1. 1915.	9035 Pte T JEFFERISS rejoins and returns to duty. C.H.	
Aug 4. 1915.	Capt C HARTLEY A.V.C. T.F. resumed command of the Nth. Mid. Mob. Vety. Section. C.H.	
Sept 20. 1915.	902 Sgt. W HAYGARTH transferred to 138th S.f.f. Bgde. C.H.	
Sept 20. 1915.	9047 Corpl W BRAHAM promoted to L/Sgt (temporary) and transferred to 139th S.f. Bgde. C.H.	
Sept 20. 1915.	No 199 Pte H DAWSON & 90165 Pte P EDWARDS promoted to be Corporals. C.H.	
Sept 20. 1915.	9031 Pte G HOLLIS & 91634 Pte B BRAIN transferred to Nth Mid. Mobile Vety Section from 138 & 139 Inf Bgdes. C.H.	

C. Hartley
Capt Amt F.
Nth Mid Mob Vety Section

Army Form C. 2118.

WAR DIARY
or
INTELLIGENCE SUMMARY.   1/1st N.M. Mobile Vety Section
(Erase heading not required.)

Instructions regarding War Diaries and Intelligence Summaries are contained in F. S. Regs., Part II. and the Staff Manual respectively. Title pages will be prepared in manuscript.

Hour, Date, Place	Summary of Events and Information	Remarks and references to Appendices
March 1. 1916	1/1st N.M. Mob Vety Section billeted at FIENVILLERS C.H.	
" 6. 1916	Marched to LE CAUROY C.H.	
" 11. 1916	Marched to CAMBLAIN L'ABBÉ C.H.	
" 12. 1916	Marched to MINGOVAL C.H.	
" 13. 1916	N.M. 166 Pte F Thorne & N.M. 145 Pte J. Heath join section from England. C.H.	
" 16. 1916	Horse Ambulance received in lieu of 2nd L.G.S Limbered Wagon C.H.	
" 17. 1916	Ptes. Bruce, Chell & Faires join section from England C.H.	
" 23. 1916	Sgt. E. Jones attached to 46th D.A.C., Pte. S. Skelton & Sefferies promoted to Sgts (Temp) and attached to 76th D.A.C. Corpl P. Edwards promoted to be Sergeant C.H.	
" 25. 1916	Corpl S.G. Vine Joins Section from Depot 46th Division on	
" 28. 1916	Lieut J. Facet A.V.C takes over temporary command	

Army Form C. 2118.

WAR DIARY
or
INTELLIGENCE SUMMARY.
(Erase heading not required.)

Hqrs N.M. Middle Kty Section Vol 17

Place	Date	Hour	Summary of Events and Information	Remarks and references to Appendices
Nœux-les-Mines	1/5/17		19 animals evacuated from Nœux-les-Mines Station.	19 animals evacuated from Bethune Ky haye
	4/5/17		15 animals evacuated from Bethune Ky haye & 3 by train	
	4/5/17	8.15	Bullet killed. Horses removed from lines for night.	
	5/6/17		32 animals evacuated from Nœux-les-Mines Station.	MVS moved to Barlin.
Barlin	9/5/17		3 horses evacuated from Bethune Ky haye	
	11/5/17		8 horses evacuated from Bethune Ky haye. 10 horses evacuated from Barlin by train
	14/5/17		12 horses evacuated from Bethune Ky haye	
	15/5/17		31 horses evacuated from Barlin Station.	
	17/5/17		12 animals evacuated from Bethune Ky haye.	
	19/5/17		17 animals evacuated from Bethune Ky haye and 12 from Barlin Station	
	22/5/17		23 animals evacuated from Barlin Station.	
	24/5/17		Inspected by Director of Veterinary Services.	
	25/5/17		11 animals evacuated from Bethune Ky haye and 10 from Barlin Station	
	26/5/17		9 animals evacuated from Bethune Ky haye.	
	28/5/17		24 animals evacuated from Barlin Station.	
	30/5/17		Capt C Hartley to Lord Mayor for temporary duty as A.D.V.S. Capt T Thomson takes over temporary command of MVS. C Hartley Capt RAVC

Army Form C. 2118.

WAR DIARY
or
INTELLIGENCE SUMMARY.
(Erase heading not required.)

1/1st W.R. Mob. Vety Section

Instructions regarding War Diaries and Intelligence Summaries are contained in F.S. Regs., Part II. and the Staff Manual respectively. Title pages will be prepared in manuscript.

Hour, Date, Place	Summary of Events and Information	Remarks and references to Appendices
March 1. 1915.	Mobile Vety Section landed at LE HAVRE from S.S. Blackwell C.H.	
" 2 1915	Marechal de Logis L. BLOMBET attached as French Interpreter. C.H.	
" 5 1915	Entrained for CASSEL. C.H.	
" 9 1915	Detrained at BAVINCHOVE C.H.	
" 11 1915	14 men inoculated against Typhoid. C.H.	
" 16 1915	Marched to ROUGE CROIX, CAESTRE C.H.	
" 19 1915	Marched to SAILLY-SUR-LA-LYS. C.H.	
" 28 1915	Marched to MERRIS. C.H.	
" 28 1915	Inspected by Director of Veterinary Services. C.H.	
	14 men inoculated against Typhoid. C.H.	
	Received 7 horses to complete to establishment. C.H.	
	During these marches much difficulty was experienced as the transport which consisted of 1 G.S. Limbered Wagon proved quite inadequate	

C Hartley
Capt. A.V.C (T.F)
O.C. 1/1st W.R. Mob. Vet Sec.

Army Form C. 2118.

WAR DIARY
or
INTELLIGENCE SUMMARY.
(Erase heading not required.)

11 st N.M. Mob Vety Section

Hour, Date, Place	Summary of Events and Information	Remarks and references to Appendices
Oct 1. 1915.	11th Mid Mobile Vety Section Mobilized at 2.15. P.O.1 on Mob Sheet 24.	
Oct 3. 1915. Oct 3 1915 Oct 4 1915	Marched to Lieut BERQUIN. (Approx'd to Farriers (Regimen Sub Farriers) detached from N.N.M.V.S.) Marched to BUSNES.	
Oct 6. 1915	Marched to LABEUVRIERE. D/y & 2 Bethune Combined Fleet	
Oct 13. 1915	9048 Pte G. BRIZZLE joins 11th Mid M.V.S. from 11tt Midland Vety Hospital, Luton.	Memorandum Navy Duff Hallom 25/1/16
Oct 27. 1915.	Marched to VERQUIN. E.29.C.4.5 Bethune Combined Sheet	
Oct 8. 1915.	L/S Lapointe Schull attached to 11th Mid M.V.S.	C. Hartley Capt AVC-F. Comdg 11th N.M. Mid M.V.S.

Army Form C. 2118.

WAR DIARY
or
INTELLIGENCE SUMMARY.
(Erase heading not required.)

W/net N.M. Mot. Kelp Section

Instructions regarding War Diaries and Intelligence Summaries are contained in F.S. Regs., Part II. and the Staff Manual respectively. Title pages will be prepared in manuscript.

Hour, Date, Place	Summary of Events and Information	Remarks and references to Appendices
July 1. 1915.	11th Fld Mobile Vety Section billeted at FERME-DE-LA-BOIS, WESTOUTRE. CH	
July 16. 1915.	No 55 Private T. JEFFERIES admitted to No1 Field Ambulance 46th Division, suffering from inflamed eyesight. CH	
July 22. 1915.	Lieut JOHN FACER, A.V.C. T.F. took command of the 11th Fld Mobile Vety Section during the absence of Officer Commanding on leave to England. CH	
July 24. 1915.	19095 Pte. F. CHAPMAN evacuated sick and struck off strength of 11th Fld. Mob Vety Section. CH	
July 24. 1915.	Demonstration by Lieut. F. HOBDAY, A.V.C. on the Subcutaneous Palpebral method of Mallenisation of horses. CH	
July 29. 1915.	Marched to billet on POPERINGHE-ABEELE Rd. L.15. d. 8. 1 on High sheet 27. CH	

C. Hartley
Capt. A.V.C. (T.F.)
Cmndg 11th F. Mob. V. S.

William ... (signature)

WAR DIARY
or
INTELLIGENCE SUMMARY.
(Erase heading not required.)

Army Form C. 2118.

46

1/1st (A.M.) MOBILE
VETERINARY SECTION.
48th DIVISION.
No. ....
Date 31-12-18

Place	Date	Hour	Summary of Events and Information	Remarks and references to Appendices
Infield	2/12/18		Sgt Winter journey home 14 days	
	3/12/18		Evacuated 32 horses to XIII VES	
	4/12/18		Received 3 mules to XIII VES. No Cavalry Hospital in Arm	
	7/12/18		Evacuated 6 horses to XIII VES	
	8/12/18		Evacuated 8 horses to XIII VES	
	9/12/18		Received 11 horses VES. Pte Bull admitted sick	
	10/12/18		Evacuated 30 horses to XIII VES (25 from HENRYS)	
	11/12/18		Evacuated 8 horses to XIII VES	
	13/12/18		Evacuated 16 " " XIII VES	
	14/12/18		Evacuated 11 " " XIII VES	
	16/12/18		Evacuated 24 horses " XIII VES	
	20/12/18		Evacuated 8 horses " XIII VES	
	21/12/18		Evacuated 11 horses " XIII VES Pte Handy difficult road to hospital & Returned	
	24/12/18		Evacuated 9 horses " XIII VES	
	28/12/18		Evacuated 32 horses " XIII VES	
	29/12/18		Evacuated	

Army Form C. 2118.

WAR DIARY
or
INTELLIGENCE SUMMARY.
(Erase heading not required.)

Instructions regarding War Diaries and Intelligence Summaries are contained in F. S. Regs., Part II. and the Staff Manual respectively. Title pages will be prepared in manuscript.

"A" Cettain C. Hartley
Commanding N°G N°T?
Commanding N° 46 Field M.V.S

Vol 16

Place	Date	Hour	Summary of Events and Information	Remarks and references to Appendices
FONTES	1/4/17		Marched to FONTES. Men and horses finished the march in good condition and without casualties. Conducting festas of 24/3/17 & 28/3/17 agrees and	
	2/4/17		Four men of N°46 & T.M. Batty returned to their unit.	
			24 horses evacuated from LILLERS.	
			7614 & 10 Street ones & infants as per line transport sheet A.S.C.	
	6/4/17		55 animals evacuated from LILLERS.	
	10/4/17		39 animals evacuated from LILLERS. 5 infantry men returned to N° 3 N.M. Field Ambulance.	
BIGNES	13/4/17		Moved to BOGNES. 38 animals evacuated from LILLERS.	
"	17/4/17		23 animals evacuated from LILLERS. 2 horse vans of N°506 A.S.C. sent down to N°36 M.V.S. for evacuation	
NOEUX-LES-MINES	23/4/17		Moved to NOEUX-LES-MINES taking over from N°36 M.V.S.	
			Settled in very good condition	
"	25/4/17		Eaton horses put through dipping bath at BARLIN	
"	29/4/17		56 animals evacuated from NOEUX-LES-MINES.	

C Hartley Capt N°46 T.
H.M N.M N°46 Vety Section

2353 Wt. W3544/1454 700,000 5/15 D. D. & L. A.D.S.S./Forms/C. 2118.

WAR DIARY
or
INTELLIGENCE SUMMARY.
(Erase heading not required.)

Army Form C. 2118.

1/1st Nth. Mid. Mobile Vety Section

Hour, Date, Place	Summary of Events and Information	Remarks and references to Appendices
Dec 1st 1915.	1/1st Nth Mid Mobile Vety Section billeted at LE BOUZATEUR F.M.E. 9th day Bethune Combined Sheet. C.M.	
Dec 5th 1915	Marched to LA HAYE ST VENANT C.M.	
Dec 10th 1915	Inspected by L.O.C. A.D. 6th Division C.M.	
Dec 16th 1915	90125 Pte A.S. Russell evacuated to L.O.C. to report to D.D.M.S. ROUEN C.M.	
Dec 19th 1915	Marched to THIENNES. I.16.a.8.8. Sheet 36A C.M.	
Dec 25th 1915	Cpl. H. Dawson no 99 attached to 139th Inf Bgde as Sergeant (temp) C.M. Pte. H. Garbutt no 100 promoted to Cpl oral (temp) C.M.	

C Hunter
Captain (F.)
Comdg 1/1st N.M.M.V.S.

WAR DIARY or INTELLIGENCE SUMMARY

Army Form C. 2118.

1/1st N.M. Mobile Vety Station

Place	Date	Hour	Summary of Events and Information	Remarks and references to Appendices
LARBERT	1/9/16		16 sick animals evacuated from LARBERT Station.	
	3/9/16		16 sick animals evacuated from LARBERT Station.	
	6/9/16		18 sick animals evacuated from LARBERT Station.	
	9/9/16		38 sick animals evacuated from LARBERT Station.	
	11/9/16		N.M.222 Pte JERVIS A.V.C. transf. from 3rd Army School of Cookery. N.M.262 Pte HARBER proceeds to 40th Div School of Sanitation.	
	12/9/16		49 animals cast for Remount: recons by D.D.V. 3rd Army and 16 sick animals evacuated from LARBERT Station.	
	13/9/16		27 sick animals evacuated from LARBERT Station. N.M.262 Pte E. HARBER regains from 40th Div School of Sanitation.	
	16/9/16		43 cast & D.D.V 3rd Army. N.M.16 Pte T. BUTTLE A.V.C &	
	18/9/16		49 sick animals evacuated from LARBERT Station. N.M 62 Cpl. H. McCARTHY regains	
			N.M.22 Pte. W. GREEN A.V.C. evacuated sick from No 2. B.V.H.	
	21/9/16		11 sick animals evacuated from LARBERT Station.	
	23/9/16		30 sick animals evacuated from LARBERT Station.	
	24/9/16		N.M. 175 Pte ST HEATH A.V.C. evacuated sick. During the month the floor of an existing shed for 24 horses has been made good – Rebuilt for 16 horses built according to 4th Corps plans and given a concrete floor. A Lean-to shed capable of holding some 12 horses has also been erected. Much work has also been done to improve the sanitation & general comfort of the billet which is reasonable for all N.M. & H.I. Level as at all close to Falkirk and on a main road.	

C. Hoitt Cpt. AVC
Comdg NM M.V. Sn.

Army Form C. 2118.

WAR DIARY
or
INTELLIGENCE SUMMARY.
(Erase heading not required.)

Instructions regarding War Diaries and Intelligence Summaries are contained in F. S. Regs., Part II. and the Staff Manual respectively. Title pages will be prepared in manuscript.

Place	Date	Hour	Summary of Events and Information	Remarks and references to Appendices
In field	23/10/18		Mb.V.S. moved to Fresney le Grand Evacuated 26 to IX V.E.S.	
	24/10/18		Evacuated 16 horses to IX V.E.S.	
	25/10/18		Pt Wilkin granted 14 days leave to U.K. 26/10/18 - 9/11/18 Evacuated 16 horses to IX V.E.S.	
	29/10/18		Evacuated 13 horses to IX V.E.S.	
	30/10/18		Evacuated 17 horses to IX V.E.S.	
	31/10/18		Mb.V.S. moved to Bohain Evacuated 2 horses to IX V.E.S.	

Johnston
Capt AVGT.

1/1st (CIM) MOBILE
VETERINARY SECTION.
46TH DIVISION.
No 31/10/16

WAR DIARY
or
INTELLIGENCE SUMMARY.
(Erase heading not required.)

Army Form C. 2118.

No 1 N.M. Mob. Vety Section

Hour, Date, Place	Summary of Events and Information	Remarks and references to Appendices

Jan 1st 1916 — No 1 N.M. Mob. Vety. Section billeted at THIENNES Z.16.a.8.8. Sht 36a. C.H.

Jan 3rd 1916 — Marched to LAMBRES M.10.B.6.2. Sheet 36a C.H.

Jan 24th 1916 — No 124 Pte W Cavenet evacuated sick to No 2 C.C.S. at AIRE C.H.

Jan 26th 1916 — Entrained at BERGUETTE Station for PONT-REMY Station arriving 9 p.m. Marched to

Jan 27th 1916 — VILLERS-SOUS-AILLY C.H.

WAR DIARY
or
INTELLIGENCE SUMMARY.
(Erase heading not required.)

1/1st N.M. Mob. Vety Section

Army Form C. 2118.

Hour, Date, Place	Summary of Events and Information	Remarks and references to Appendices
June 1. 1915.	9th Mtd. Mobile Vety Section billeted at Ferme de La-Bourse, Bailleul. CH	
2. 1915	Privates HODGKISS J, GREEN W, EDWARDS P, DAWSON T, GARBUTT H, JEFFERIS T, WESTON A, FORSTER G, FOSTER P, CAVENOR W, BUTTLE T, HOWELL C, RUSSELL A.S, BILLINGTON H, LATHAM E, CHAPMAN F, GOODE B. given 6d per day Corps Pay to take effect from March 1. 1915. CH	
June 18. 1915	No 5 Sgt F.J. EAMES evacuated to England and struck off strength of NR 9Mrd. M.V.S. CH	
June 26. 1915.	Marched to FERME DE-LA-BOIS, WESTOUTRE. CH	

C. Hartley
Capt. A.V.C.(T.F.)
Comdg N°1 9th Mtd Fld M.V.S.

Montague Fletcher
Lieut-Colonel
Commanding...

Army Form C. 2118.

WAR DIARY
or
INTELLIGENCE SUMMARY.   1/1st N.M. Mot Vol Section
(Erase heading not required.)

Instructions regarding War Diaries and Intelligence Summaries are contained in F.S. Regs., Part II. and the Staff Manual respectively. Title pages will be prepared in manuscript.

Hour, Date, Place	Summary of Events and Information	Remarks and references to Appendices
April 6. 1915	Marched to FERME-DE-LA-BOURSE. BAILLEUL C.H.	
" 18. 1915	M de L COLCOMBET (French Interpreter) detached from N.M. M.V.S. C.H.	
" 19. 1915	S/Sgmst G. FANNING (Belgian Interpreter) attached to N.M. M.V.S. C.H.	

Forwarded
Willoughby

C. Hartley
Capt AVC (TF)
Commanding 1/1st N Mid. Md. V. S.

Vol/3

Army Form C. 2118.

WAR DIARY
or
INTELLIGENCE SUMMARY.
(Erase heading not required.)

Instructions regarding War Diaries and Intelligence Summaries are contained in F. S. Regs., Part II. and the Staff Manual respectively. Title pages will be prepared in manuscript.

#4 N.M. Mobile Vety Section

Place	Date	Hour	Summary of Events and Information	Remarks and references to Appendices
CRINCOURT	1/1/17		31 animals evacuated from WARINCOURT.	10/1/17 Pte Clarke W.W. to Hos/124 PG
			SURGINCON R. A.V.C. 7+ joined from No 2 Vety Hospital	
	9/1/17		40 animals evacuated from WARINCOURT.	
	13/1/17		31 animals evacuated from WARINCOURT	
	17/1/17		29 animals evacuated from WARINCOURT	
	22/1/17		26 animals evacuated from WARINCOURT	
	26/1/17		24 animals evacuated from WARINCOURT	
			Evacuation of animals by rail impeded owing to congestion of traffic. Before this time some trouble had been experienced, the Conducting parties being delayed on their return journeys. The majority of the animals evacuated this month have been cases of Contagious Skin Disease.	

C Harker
Capt AVC
1/2/17

Headquarters
46th (North) Division
Forwarded
[signature]
D.D.V.S. 46th North Div.
1/2/17

Army Form C. 2118.

WAR DIARY
or
INTELLIGENCE SUMMARY.
(Erase heading not required.)

1/1st N.M. Mob Vety Section

Instructions regarding War Diaries and Intelligence Summaries are contained in F. S. Regs., Part II. and the Staff Manual respectively. Title pages will be prepared in manuscript.

Hour, Date, Place	Summary of Events and Information	Remarks and references to Appendices
Nov 1. 1915	1/1st Nth. Mid. Mobile Vety Section billeted at E.29.c.4.5. Bethune Combined Sheet. C.H.	
Nov 7. 1915	90.208 Pte W.C. Brown joined from 11th Mob Vety Hospital Section C.H.	
Nov 7. 1915	Marched to LA FOSSE R.22.a.8.y. Bethune Combined Sheet C.H.	
Nov 16. 1915	Marched to LE BOUZATEUX M.5 D.11.d.8.y. C.H.	
Nov 24. 1915	Inspected by G.O.C. 11th Corps. C.H.	

C Huntley
Capt AVC(T.F.)
Comdg 1/1st 1st Mid Mob V.S.

WAR DIARY
or
INTELLIGENCE SUMMARY.
(Erase heading not required.)

Army Form C. 2118.

Nov 45

Place	Date	Hour	Summary of Events and Information	Remarks and references to Appendices
Field	1/10/18	—	Evacuated 367 horses to IX V.E.S.	
	2/10/18		Evacuated 37 horses to IX V.E.S	
	3/10/18		Evacuated 31 horses to IX V.E.S.	
	4/10/18		Evacuated 32 horses to IX V.E.S.	
	5/10/18		Evacuated 31 horses to IX V.E.S.	
	6/10/18		Pte. Cluffe granted 14 days leave to UK 9/10/18 - 23/10/18	
	7/10/18		Evacuated 28 horses to IX V.E.S.	
	8/10/18		Evacuated 42 horses to IX V.E.S.	
	9/10/18		Evacuated 21 horses to IX V.E.S.	
	10/10/18		Evacuated 9 horses to IX V.E.S. No. V.S. moved to Bellenglise	
	11/10/18		No. V.S. moved to Seguehart	
	13/10/18		Evacuated 25 horses for 2 No. V.S	
	15/10/18		Evacuated 11 horses to IX V.E.S	
	17/10/18		Lt. Coss granted 14 days leave to UK 19/10/18 - 2/11/18 Evacuated 40 horses	
	23/10/18		Lt. Slingsby granted 14 days leave to UK 23/10/18 - 5/11/18 Advanced post sent to Fresnoy-le-Grand	

Army Form C. 2118.

46

WAR DIARY
or
INTELLIGENCE SUMMARY.
(Erase heading not required.)

1/1st N.M. Mobile Vety Section

Place	Date	Hour	Summary of Events and Information	Remarks and references to Appendices
MINGOVAL	4/4/16		N/M 124 Pte W Lavenet rejoins unit	
"	6/4/16		31 horses evacuated from AUBIGNY STATION	
"	9/4/16		16 " " " "	
"	10/4/16		Inspection by D.D.V. 3rd Army of animals prepared for casting for remount reasons.	
"	12/4/16		18 remount cases and 7 sick animals evacuated from AUBIGNY.	
"	13/4/16		Capt Hartley resumes command	
"	17/4/16		39 horses evacuated from AUBIGNY Station.	
"	20/4/16		25 " " " "	
"	22/4/16		13 " " " "	
"	23/4/16		Move to ROELLECOURT to billets vacated by M.V.S. of 23rd Division	
"	25/4/16		17 horses evacuated from Pet Vet Station. Capt Hartley proceeds to England on leave of absence. Capt J Facer A.V.C. T. taken over command.	
"	26/4/16		N/M 42 Pte Sykes transferred to unit from 45th Div Hqrs.	
"	27/4/16		N/M 19 Pte S Wells, N/M 29036 Chesire, N/M 28036 Harber A.V.C.T. join unit from England. 34 horses evacuated from P.V.St.	
"	29/4/16		19 men inoculated with mixed Typhoid Vaccine	

C Hartley Capt A.V.C.

Mob Vety See

Vol 21

WAR DIARY
or
INTELLIGENCE SUMMARY.
(Erase heading not required.)

Army Form C. 2118.

Instructions regarding War Diaries and Intelligence Summaries are contained in F.S. Regs., Part II. and the Staff Manual respectively. Title pages will be prepared in manuscript.

Place	Date	Hour	Summary of Events and Information	Remarks and references to Appendices
Brown	Sept 1		14 horses evacuated (barge)	
	2		21 horses evacuated (train)	
	5		8 horses evacuated (barge)	
	7		24 horses evacuated (train) eight cast by D.D.V.T Army	
	11		18 horses evacuated (barge)	
	14		24 horses evacuated (barge)	
	15		Pte Saunders 10 days leave	
	16		Pte McSherry 10 days leave	
	17		4 horses evacuated (barge)	
	18		Evacuation of two eight Thoms by G.O.C. 46 Dn.	
	20		F/Sgt Brown 10 days leave	
	21		18 horses evacuated (barge)	
	22		Pte SAP man 10 days leave	
	23		16 horses evacuated (train)	
	24		Pte Miller 10 days leave	
	25		17 horses evacuated (barge) Dr J.H.Day A.S.C. transferred 2nd Battalion Rifle Brigade A.O.204 1/6 Authority B.R. 66974. 2dGs officer leave Reason for Transfer Benefit of Service and own request	
	28		8 horses evacuated (barge)	
	29		Dr Slingsby 10 days leave	

John Facer
Capt AVCTF
11th NM Mobile Veterinary Section

Army Form C. 2118.

WAR DIARY
or
INTELLIGENCE SUMMARY.
(Erase heading not required.)

1/1st N.M. Mob. Vety. Section

Hour, Date, Place	Summary of Events and Information	Remarks and references to Appendices
Jan. 1st 1916	1/1st N.M. Mob. Vety. Section billetted at THIENNES I. 16.a.8.8. Sheet 36a. CH.	
Jan. 3rd 1916.	Marched to LAMBRES N.10.2.8.2. Sheet 36a. CH.	
Jan. 24th 1916	No. 124 Pte W. Everenot evacuated sick to 22 C.C.S. at AIRE, CH.	
Jan. 26th 1916	Entrained at BERGUETTE Station for PONT-REMY Station arriving 9 p.m. Marched to	
Jan 27th 1916	VILLERS-SOUS-AILLY CH.	

C Hartley
Capt. AVC

Army Form C. 2118.

WAR DIARY
or
INTELLIGENCE SUMMARY.
(Erase heading not required.)

Instructions regarding War Diaries and Intelligence Summaries are contained in F. S. Regs., Part II. and the Staff Manual respectively. Title pages will be prepared in manuscript.

Place	Date	Hour	Summary of Events and Information	Remarks and references to Appendices
Sufed	24/1/19		Evacuated 6 animals to XII V.E.S.	
	25/1/19		" 18 " " " "	
	26/1/19		" 11 " " " "	
	28/1/19		" 16 " " " "	
	29/1/19		" 12 " " " "	
	30/1/19		" 7 " " " "	
	31/1/19		" 13 " " " "	

John Facer
Capt. A.V.C. E.F.

1/1st (W.M.) MOBILE
VETERINARY SECTION.
48th DIVISION.
No.............
Date............

WAR DIARY
or
INTELLIGENCE SUMMARY.
(Erase heading not required.)

Army Form C. 2118.

1/1st (D.M.) MOBILE VETERINARY SECTION, 40th DIVISION.

Place	Date	Hour	Summary of Events and Information	Remarks and references to Appendices
April	13/2/19		Evacuated 4 animals to XII. V.E.S.	
	19/2/19		" 15 " " "	
	20/2/19		No V.S. moved to Le Cateau	
	25/2/19		Evacuated 8 animals to XIII V.E.S.	
	26/2/19		" 10 " " "	
	27/2/19		" 8 " " "	
	28/2/19		" 6 " " "	

John Faen
J. Cap RAVC TF

WAR DIARY or INTELLIGENCE SUMMARY

Army Form C. 2118.

1/1 N.M. Fmn Fd. Amb[?] W.ef Sec

Place	Date	Hour	Summary of Events and Information	Remarks and references to Appendices
In field	1/11/18		Evacuated 19 horses to IX V.E.S.	
	3/11/18		Evacuated 9 horses to IX V.E.S.	
	4/11/18		Evacuated 20 horses to IX V.E.S.	
	6/11/18		M.V.S. moved to L'Isle de Gunes	
	6/11/18		Evacuated 11 horses to IX V.E.S.	
	7/11/18		M.V.S. moved to Catillon. Evacuated 7 horses to IX V.E.S.	
	8/11/18		M.V.S. moved to Prisches. Evacuated 16 horses to 2nd M.V.S. advanced post	
	9/11/18		Advanced post sent to Boulogne sur Helpe. Evacuated 17 horses to 2 M.V.S.	
	11/11/18		Evacuated 1 horse to 2nd M.V.S. and 6 from 7th M.V.S. Pte Welsh[?] Fowns[?] return off leave.	
	13/11/18		M.V.S. moved to Landrecies	
	14/11/18		Evacuated 18 horses to XIII V.E.S.	
	15/11/18		Evacuated 42 horses to XIII V.E.S. (28 from 1/1 E. & horses 16 V.S. 14 from 1/1 N.M. M.V.S.)	
	16/11/18		Sergt Edwards proceeds on leave to England 18/11/18 to 1/12/18	
	18/11/18		Evacuated 29 horses to XIII V.E.S. (11 from 1/1 E. horses M.V.S.)	
	19/11/18		Evacuated 39 horses to XIII V.E.S. (18 from 1/1 E. horses M.V.S.)	

Army Form C. 2118.

WAR DIARY
or
INTELLIGENCE SUMMARY.
(Erase heading not required.)

1/1st N.M. Mob. Vety Section

Instructions regarding War Diaries and Intelligence Summaries are contained in F. S. Regs., Part II. and the Staff Manual respectively. Title pages will be prepared in manuscript.

Hour, Date, Place	Summary of Events and Information	Remarks and references to Appendices
May 1. 1915.	7th Mtd. Mobile Vety Section billeted at FERME-6-14. BOURSE, BARLEUR. CH	
May 15. 1915.	T34813 Driver J.A. DAY. Army Service Corps attached as 1st line transport driver. CH	
May 15. 1915.	2 mules and 1 G.S. limbered wagon received to complete to establishment. CH	

C. Hartley
Capt AVC (T)
Comdg 1/1st N. Mid Mob Vet Sec

WAR DIARY
or
INTELLIGENCE SUMMARY

(Erase heading not required.)

Army Form C. 2118.

Place	Date	Hour	Summary of Events and Information	Remarks and references to Appendices
In the Field	12/1/17		Column moved from GREVAS to HENU	MP
	13/1/17		Lt. K. ROACH from 2nd Cavalry Supply Column to replace Lt. W.H.M. HIGHAM	MP
	6/1/17		T/2nd Lt W.H.M. HIGHAM to Headquarter Canteen	MP
	27/1/17		75 tons of coal from BRUAY	MP
	28/1/17		50 tons of coal from BRUAY	MP
	31/1/17		Instructions received for Major W.A. POTTER to take command of VII Corps Supply Column on re-organisation of M.T., authority letter Q.M.G. Wo. ASC/11870. Command of No 465 supply Column handed over to T/Capt. J.D. MITCHELL	MP

W.A. Potter Major
OC No 465 SC

WAR DIARY
INTELLIGENCE SUMMARY
(Erase heading not required.)

Army Form C. 2118.

1/1st N.M. Mobile Vety Section.

Place	Date	Hour	Summary of Events and Information	Remarks and references to Appendices
GRINCOURT	1/3/17		35 animals evacuated from WARINCOURT	
	5/3/17		Section horses paced through dipping bath as precautionary measure.	
	9/3/17		Capt C. HARTLEY A.V.C.T. assumes command.	
	10/3/17		Roads around this billet are impassable for Horse Ambulance.	
	20/3/17		31 animals evacuated from WARINCOURT	
	24/3/17		8 men attached temporarily to act as conducting party. 112 horses evacuated from WARINCOURT.	
	27/3/17		40 animals evacuated from BELLE EGLISE	
	28/3/17		96 animals evacuated from WARINCOURT	
	29/3/17		34 animals evacuated from WARINCOURT Four men attached from V & 6 Heavy T.M. Batty to form part of conducting party.	
MEZEROLLES	29/3/17		Unit marched to MEZEROLLES via DOULLENS following B Echelon 46th D.A.C. under orders of P.D.C.R.A. 46th Divn.	
MONCHEL	30/3/17		Marched to MONCHEL. Road very bad from FROHEN LE GRAND to VIEUX L'HOPITAL.	
ANVIN	31/3/17		Marched to ANVIN. Violent Hailstorm whilst leaving MONCHEL.	

C. Hartley Capt. A.V.C.
Commanding 1/1 N.M. F.V. Sectn.

Forwarded
Witheringham Oh 1st vety Secn
2/4/17

WAR DIARY
or
INTELLIGENCE SUMMARY.
(Erase heading not required.)

Army Form C. 2118.

Mob Vety Sec

Place	Date	Hour	Summary of Events and Information	Remarks and references to Appendices
Field	2/1/19		Evacuated 5 animals to XVII V.E.S	
	4/1/19		" " 5 " " "	
	6/1/19		" " 7 " " "	
	7/1/19		" " 21 " " "	
	8/1/19		" " 6 " " "	
	9/1/19		" " 15 " " "	
	10/1/19		" " 12 " " "	
	11/1/19		" " 10 " " "	
	13/1/19		" " 24 " " "	
	15/1/19		" " 20 " " "	
	16/1/19		" " 15 " " "	
	17/1/19		" " 7 " " "	
	19/1/19		" " 5 " " "	
	21/1/19		" " 38 " " "	
	22/1/19		" " 5 " " "	
	23/1/19		" " 14 " " "	

WAR DIARY of Captain C Hartley AVC(T) 1/1st N.M. Mobile Vety Section
or
INTELLIGENCE SUMMARY

Army Form C. 2118.

(Erase heading not required)

Vol 10

Place	Date	Hour	Summary of Events and Information	Remarks and references to Appendices
LARBRET	1/10/16		N.M. 125 C/S/Corporal Q.S. Russell A.V.C.T. rejoins from course of instruction on clipping at 902 B.V.H.	
	5/10/16		29 animals evacuated from LARBRET STATION.	
			N.M. 232 Pte J Titterton AVCT joins from 9102 BVH. N.M. 155 Pte Clatham promoted to Corp. C/S/Q/R/St and attached to A/280 Bgde R.F.A.	
	7/10/16		4 animals evacuated from LARBRET STATION	
	10/10/16		N.M. 82 C/S/Corporal McCarthy evacuated sick.	
	11/10/16		31 animals evacuated from LARBRET STATION	
	14/10/16		21 " " " " "	
	17/10/16		29 " " " " " . N.M 97 Pte W Green AVCT joins from 9102 B.V.H.	
	18/10/16		N.M. 97. Pte H Senior A.V.C.T joins from 9102 BVH	
	22/10/16		33 animals evacuated from LARBRET STATION.	
	26/10/16		N.M 232 Pte J Titterton AVCT evacuated sick.	
	27/10/16		18 animals & 16 animals cast by D.D.V. 3rd Army evacuated from LARBRET STATION. 16 animals evacuated from LARBRET. Handed over billet at LARBRET to 970 & O.M.V.S. leaving one sick horse.	
	30/10/16			
COCOCHES	31/10/16		Marched to COCOCHES via DOULLENS, leaving at 8.30 am and arriving at 3 p.m.	

Headquarters
1/1 M Mobile V.S.

Forwarded
C Hartley
Captain

C Hartley
Captain

3/11/16 ADSS

WAR DIARY
or
INTELLIGENCE SUMMARY.
(Erase heading not required.)

Army Form C. 2118.

1/1st (N.M.) MOBILE VETERINARY SECTION, 46TH DIVISION.

Feb 49

Place	Date	Hour	Summary of Events and Information	Remarks and references to Appendices
Oujed	3/2/19		Evacuated 4 animals to XIII V.E.S.	
	4/2/19		7 " " " " "	
	5/2/19		17 " " " " "	
	6/2/19		4 " " " " "	
	7/2/19		4 " " " " "	
	8/2/19		12 " " " " "	
	9/2/19		9 " " " " "	
	10/2/19		2 " " " " "	
	11/2/19		3 " " " " "	
	12/2/19		7 " " " " " Pte Jones granted 14 days leave to UK	
	13/2/19		12 " " " " "	
	14/2/19		10 " " " " "	
	15/2/19		" Pte Hayes Evans granted 14 days leave	
	16/2/19		7 " " " " " Pte Rickaby granted 14 days leave to UK	
	17/2/19		Evacuated 3 animals to VES.	

WAR DIARY or INTELLIGENCE SUMMARY

Army Form C. 2118.

Mot Vety Sec / Veterinary

Place	Date	Hour	Summary of Events and Information	Remarks and references to Appendices
In field	4/9/18		Evacuated 6 horses to X V.E.S.	
	7/9/18		Pte Hodson & Corpl Chubin proceed on 14 days leave	
	8/9/18		Pte Hardy proceeds on leave. Captain att F.A. Capt T Tompson takes over command	
	9/9/18		Evacuated 3 horses to I V.E.S.	
	12/9/18		M.V.S. entrained at Ticher for Heilly. Pte Palmer proceed on leave	
	15/9/18		Captain returns to M.V.S.	
	16/9/18		Evacuated 6 horses to III V.E.S.	
	18/9/18		Handed over 8 horses to 42nd M.V.S.	
	19/9/18		M.V.S. moved to Townsville. Handed over 5 + 2 to 42 & M.V.S.	
	20/9/18		M.V.S. moved to Morn en Chausée	
	21/9/18		Pte Allen & Pte Hadow return from leave	
	22/9/18		Evacuated 9 horses to IX V.E.S	
	23/9/18		Pte Hodson & Corpl Chubin return from leave	
	24/9/18		Corpl Chubin deputed to 2 V.H. Evacuated 4 horses to IX V.E.S	
	26/9/18		Evacuated 9 horses to IX V.E.S. Sgt Hardy returning from leave	
			Advanced post open at Vraignes (1 N.C.O 1 man)	
	27/9/18		Evacuated 13 horses to IX V.E.S. Rec'd 16 from advanced post	
	29/9/18		Pte Hinchcliffe proceeds on leave. Pte Palmer returned to unit	
			Evacuated 9 to IX V.E.S.	
	30/9/18		moves to Vraidier M.V.S.	

J Whitever
Capt AVC TF

Army Form C. 2118.

WAR DIARY
or
INTELLIGENCE SUMMARY.
(Erase heading not required.)

1/1st N.M. Mobile Vety. Sect.

Place	Date	Hour	Summary of Events and Information	Remarks and references to Appendices
BARLIN	17/6/17		Evacuated 15 horses by barge. 1 to 23 Vety. Hospital	
	19/6/17		7.0.T. 03032 Pte Clarke M.M. A.V.C. evacuated sick from 1/2nd N.M Field Ambulance	
	21/6/17		Evacuated 8 horses for Mange to 23 Vety. Hospital	
	22/6/17		9 Horses evacuated by Barge	
	23/6/17		Evacuated 16 horses including 8 mange cases	
	24/6/17		Rifle & kit inspection	
	25/6/17		5 Horses evacuated by Barge; and 2 Mange cases by train from BETHUNE	
	26/6/17		Evacuated 8 mange cases	
	27/6/17		Capt. HARTLEY returned from leave and takes over duty as D.A.D.V.S. Division. C.M. RUSSEL in charge of 3 men from an advanced post at BULLY GRENAY.	
	28/6/17		Evacuated 11 horses by Barge.	
	29/6/17		Evacuated 8 cases of Mange.	

1/1st (N.M.) MOBILE
VETERINARY SECTION,
46TH DIVISION.

No. V 175-
Date 30/6/17

J. Thomson
Capt. A.V.C.(J)
O.C. 1/1st N.M. M.V.S.

Army Form C. 2118.

WAR DIARY
or
INTELLIGENCE SUMMARY.
(Erase heading not required.)

Instructions regarding War Diaries and Intelligence Summaries are contained in F. S. Regs., Part II. and the Staff Manual respectively. Title pages will be prepared in manuscript.

Place	Date	Hour	Summary of Events and Information	Remarks and references to Appendices
In field	21/11/18		Evacuated 65 horses to XIII V.E.S (20 from M.2. 10/11/18t Bde 45 42 M.V.S)	
	22/11/18		Evacuated 37 horses to XIII V.E.S. (14 from 11th N.M.V.S) Pte Bell evacuated to hospital	
	22/11/18		Evacuated 3 horses to V.E.S	
	23/11/18		Evacuated 22 horses to XIII V.E.S (15 from 11th N.M.V.S)	
	25/11/18		Evacuated 5 animal to XIII V.E.S. Pte Bell returns from G.G.S	
	26/11/18		Evacuated 16 horses to XIII V.E.S.	
	28/11/18		Evacuated 27 horses to XIII V.E.S (10 from 11th N.M.V.S)	
	29/11/18		Pte Chapple sent to hospital	

1/1st (N.M.) MOBILE
VETERINARY SECTION.
48TH DIVISION.
No 2/12/18

Johnston
Capt A.V.C. T.F.

Army Form C. 2118.

1/1 NM Mot Vety Sec

V51 22

WAR DIARY
or
INTELLIGENCE SUMMARY.
(Erase heading not required.)

Instructions regarding War Diaries and Intelligence Summaries are contained in F. S. Regs. Part II. and the Staff Manual respectively. Title pages will be prepared in manuscript.

Place	Date	Hour	Summary of Events and Information	Remarks and references to Appendices
	Oct 1		Lt. T. Hardy attached to M.V.S. from 457 Co. A.S.C.	
	2/10/17		Evacuated 16 horses train	
	3/10/17		Evacuated 10 horses barge	
	5/10/17		Evacuated 15 horses barge 8 train	
	6/10/17		Inspection by D.V.S.	
	10/10/17		Evacuated 24 horses train including 17 cast by D.D.V. I Army. M.V.S. moved to Bethune	
	12/10/17		Evacuated 14 horse barge. One cpl and 3 men detached to Corps V.A. Detachment	
	14/10/17		Nine reinforcements received to replace 9 men dispatched to 2 V.H. on 15th	
	15/10/17		Evacuated 8 horses barge	
	19/10/17		Evacuated 167 horses barge	
	23/10/17		Evacuated 14 horses barge	
	27/10/17		Evacuated 28 horses barge	
	31/10/17		Evacuated 13 horses barge.	

John Facer
Capt A.V.C. T.F.
1/1st N.M. Mobile Veterinary Section.
1/4/17.

1/1st (N.M.) MOBILE
VETERINARY SECTION,
46TH DIVISION.
No.............
Date............

WAR DIARY or INTELLIGENCE SUMMARY.

Army Form C. 2118.

(Erase heading not required.)

Not Vety See Vol 20

Place	Date	Hour	Summary of Events and Information	Remarks and references to Appendices
Rouen	1-8-17		T.T. 02431 Private G. Harkin leave to England.	
	2-8-17		Capt. J. Facer leave to England. Capt. F. Southwark takes over Command of M.V.S. Evacuated 22 horses by Bays. 8 mangy by train.	
	3-8-17		T.T. 02430 Private Cheshire leave to England.	
	5-8-17		Evacuated 5 mangy by barge.	
	6-8-17		T.T. 31624 Private P. Walsh returned to A.S.C Depot Havre Surplus to Establishment	
	7-8-17		T.T. 02428 Private F. Palmer leave to England.	
	8-8-17		Evacuated 27 animals by Bays (including) M mangy 41 Cellulitis.	
	9-8-17		T.T. 02047 A.H. Thomas leave to England	
	10-8-17		Inspection of Horses at M.V.S. for Breeding purposes.	
	11-8-17		Entered 1/2 animals by Bays (including) 6 mdrys. 3 P.M. Examination by A.D.M.S. 4th Division for 10 Class A & 2 Class B.	
	14/8/17		Evacuated 11 horses (4 mangy) at M.V.S. Branding of brand mark Pte W.G Brown + Nayter transferred to No G. Co with effect from 13/8/17.	
	15/8/17		Evacuated 52 horses barge.	
	17/8/17		L/Cpt Kent leave to England	
	19/8/17		Cpl Poole leave to England	
	22/8/17		Evacuated 8 mangy by train	
	23/8/17		Evacuated 16 horses including 2 cast by D.D.R.1. Army Pte Sayman leave	
	24/8/17		For improvement from Z.V.H. Pte. McSharry, Nairn, Farrow returned.	
	25/8/17		Projector H 5 mm by MBMS 1 class A 4 unfit	
	28/8/17		Evacuated 19 horses barge 3 mangy	
	29/8/17		Evacuated 20 horses by Louis B mangy	

John Facer

11th N M Scottish Veterinary Section

WAR DIARY
or
INTELLIGENCE SUMMARY.

Army Form C. 2118.

46 D Mob Vety Sec

Vol 36

Place	Date	Hour	Summary of Events and Information	Remarks and references to Appendices
	4/2/18.		Evacuated eight horses (cage) Twenty eight (train) Pte. Bennett to school of Cookery.	
	5/2/18.		Pte. Dyson received a reinforcement for No 2 V.H.	
	8/2/18.		Evacuated nine horses (cage).	
	9/2/18.		Evacuated thirty two horses (train)	
	10/2/18.		1/1st N.M.V.S. moved to Boyeghem. Marching in state 1 off 23 O.R. D. Jones and Pte. Rivers 14 days leave.	
	17/2/18		Pte. Bell 14 days leave.	
	19/2/18		Pte. Somerset 14 days leave.	
	19/2/18.		Pte. Rackley + Hopner 14 days leave. Evacuated nine horses by road to 23 V.H.	
	23/2/18.		Evacuated 18 horses to 23 V.H.	
	24/2/18.		Pte. Bennett 14 days leave.	
	26/2/18.		Pte. Lightowne 14 days leave. Evacuated 8 horses to 23 V.H.	

John Ticer
Capt A.V.C. T.F.

1/1st (N.M.) MOBILE
VETERINARY SECTION,
46TH DIVISION.
No. ....
Date 28/2/18.

1/1 NM Mob Vety Sec

WAR DIARY
or
INTELLIGENCE SUMMARY.
(Erase heading not required.)

Army Form C. 2118.

Instructions regarding War Diaries and Intelligence Summaries are contained in F.S. Regs., Part II. and the Staff Manual respectively. Title pages will be prepared in manuscript.

Place	Date	Hour	Summary of Events and Information	Remarks and references to Appendices
In field	1/5/18		Evacuated 7 horses to I Corps. V.E.S.	
	2/5/18		Evacuated 16 horses to I Corps V.E.S.	
	4/5/18		Evacuated 6 horses to I Corps V.E.S.	
	6/5/18		Evacuated 10 horses to I Corps V.E.S.	
	9/5/18		Evacuated 16 horses to I Corps V.E.S.	
	11/5/18		Evacuated 5 horses to I Corps V.E.S.	
	13/5/18		Evacuated 12 horses to I Corps V.E.S.	
	15/5/18		Evacuated 5 horses to I Corps V.E.S.	
	16/5/18		Evacuated 3 horses to I Corps V.E.S.	
	19/5/18		Evacuated 14 horses to I Corps V.E.S.	
	23/5/18		Evacuated 10 horses to I Corps V.E.S.	
	25/5/18		Evacuated 9 horses to I Corps V.E.S. Nº TT0476 S/4 Staff Sergt Smyth W.E. Transferred to XCorps V.E.S. DDVS	
	27/5/18		Letter Nº 27/60/V.S. of 23/5/18	
	29/5/18		Evacuated 24 horses to I Corps V.E.S.	
	31/5/18		M.V.S. moved to Gosnay.	

J Whitacre
Capt AVC. T.

1/1st (C.E.F) MOBILE
VETERINARY SECTION,
40......
No......
Date 3/6/18.

WAR DIARY or INTELLIGENCE SUMMARY

Army Form C. 2118.

1/1st Mob Vety Sec / 7 /1/11/1918

Place	Date	Hour	Summary of Events and Information	Remarks and references to Appendices
In field	3/8/18		Evacuated Pte Lowe to 7 V.E.S	9/02 31 9/02
	4/8/18		Inspection by D.D.V.S. V Army	
	5/8/18		Evacuated 2 horses to 7 V.E.S	
	6/8/18		Evacuated 3 do do	
	7/8/18		Capt Tozer leave to England 14 days Capt Thompson takes over command	
	8/8/18		Evacuated 8 horses 7 V.E.S	
	9/8/18		Evacuated 5 do do	
	10/8/18		Evacuated 3 do do	
	11/8/18		Three returned, received Pte Shircliffe Hewitt & Welcher	
	12/8/18		Corpl Bell & Pte Ryan Nettlewood dispatched to 2 V.H.	
	13/8/18		Evacuated 6 7 V.E.S	
	14/8/18		Evacuated 6 7 V.E.S	
	15/8/18		Evacuated 8 7 V.E.S	
	16/8/18		Evacuated 6 7 V.E.S	
	17/8/18		Evacuated 4 7 V.E.S	
	19/8/18		Evacuated 9 7 V.E.S	
	20/8/18		Evacuated 3 7 V.E.S 2 V.H.	
	21/8/18		Pte Ryan returned from leave	
	22/8/18		Evacuated 3 7 V.E.S	
	23/8/18		Capt Toser returns from leave	
	24/8/18		Pte Kincutt dispatched to 2 V.H suppln to intellect	
	25/8/18		Evacuated 5 horses to 7 V.E.S T.T 02438 Pte F Thomson promoted to rank of W/A/Corpl	
	26/8/18		Evacuated 5 horses 7 V.E.S	
	27/8/18		Pte Allen returns leave to England evacuated 3 to V.E.S	
	29/8/18			
	31/8/18			

Johnson
Capt AVGTF

Army Form C. 2118.

Mob Vety Sec

VA 35

WAR DIARY
or
INTELLIGENCE SUMMARY

(Erase heading not required.)

Place	Date	Hour	Summary of Events and Information	Remarks and references to Appendices
	1/1/18		Evacuated 39 horse barge	
	6/1/18		Evacuated 35 horse barge	
	8/1/18		Staff Sgt Smith 14 days leave to England	
	11/1/18		Evacuated 34 horse barge. Capt Facer returned	
	15/1/18		Evacuated 17 horse train. Medical inspection of personnel	
	17/1/18		Evacuated 27 horse barge	
	22/1/18		Evacuated 34 horse barge	
	23/1/18		No. V.S. moved to Hooglugant	
	26/1/18		Evacuated 25 horse barge	
	29/1/18		Capt Kent dispatched to 2 V.H. Pte W.J. Kerridge arrived. Pte Charlie promoted to rank of W/o/Cpl.	

Johnston
Capt AV6 I.F.

1/1st (N.M.) MOBILE
VETERINARY SECTION.
46TH DIVISION.

Army Form C. 2118.

WAR DIARY
or
INTELLIGENCE SUMMARY.
(Erase heading not required.)

1/1st N.M. Mobile Vety Section

Vol 12

Place	Date	Hour	Summary of Events and Information	Remarks and references to Appendices
LE MARAIS	2/2/16		8 sick animals evacuated from DOULLENS	
SEE DOULLENS	3/2/16		17 sick animals evacuated from BOUQUEMAISON	
	5/2/16		12 sick animals evacuated from DOULLENS	
	6/2/16		Capt T THOMSON AVC takes command during absence on leave of Capt P HARTLEY AVC	
			Unit marched to BRINCOURT and took over billets from 1st W.R.M.V.S.	
BRINCOURT	8/2/16		19 horses evacuated from WARLINCOURT	
	12/2/16		23 horses evacuated from WARLINCOURT	
	14/2/16		16 horses taken to WARLINCOURT for evacuation. As the outlived was shelled the animals were kept at MONCHCOURT.	
	17/2/16		32 animals evacuated from WARLINCOURT	
			No 2X Pte WORSEIN to W/94 Pte H SENIOR AVC evacuated sick.	
	19/2/16		Capt C HARTLEY resumes command. 24 horses evacuated from WARLINCOURT	WARLINCOURT ~~BRIGADE~~ CN
	22/2/16		16 animals evacuated from WARLINCOURT	
	28/2/16		24 animals evacuated from WARLINCOURT	

C Hartley
Capt AVC

Army Form C. 2118.

WAR DIARY
or
INTELLIGENCE SUMMARY.

(Erase heading not required.)

1/1st N.M. Mobile Vety Sectn

Instructions regarding War Diaries and Intelligence Summaries are contained in F. S. Regs., Part II. and the Staff Manual respectively. Title pages will be prepared in manuscript.

Place	Date	Hour	Summary of Events and Information	Remarks and references to Appendices
Lemnos	29/6/16		23 Remount cases and 20 sick evacuated from LARBERT. N.M.204 Pte Cook – N.M.314 Pte Pratt – N.M.29 Pte Kemp A.V.C.T. join section from England. The civilian pattern French Ambulance issued to the unit was much used during this period. I consider it to be of a very suitable type for its work though the quality of the material and the workmanship leave much to be desired and it broke down several times.	

C. Hartley
Capt. A.V.C.
Commanding 1/1st N.M.M.V.S.

D.A.Q 3rd Echelon
Base B.E.F.

Forwarded
Welenburg Lt. Colonel
A.D.V.S. 46th (N. Mid.) Division

WAR DIARY or INTELLIGENCE SUMMARY

Army Form C. 2118.

1/1st N.M. Mobile Vety Section

Vol 7

Place	Date	Hour	Summary of Events and Information	Remarks and references to Appendices
ERINCOURT	3/4/16		26 animals evacuated from LARBRET.	
	4/4/16	9.15am	Move to ENCAMP FARM exchanging billets with 20 M.V.S. A very good billet in which many improvements had been made to adapt it for a M.V.S. An advanced collecting Post of a Corporal, one man and a GS draw out the Ambulance established in LARBRET Village.	
ENCAMP O.33 a.6 Sheet 37.C.	8/4/16		15 horses evacuated from LARBRET	
	9/4/16		NM 317 Pte Pratt evacuated sick	
	22/4/16		44 horses evacuated from LARBRET	
	23/4/16		23 " " " "	
	17/4/16		22 " " " "	
	19/4/16		Inspection by D.K.S.	
	20/4/16		31 horses evacuated from LARBRET	
	23/4/16		32 " " " "	
			sent from England.	
	24/4/16		32 horses evacuated from LARBRET	
	30/4/16		NM 316 Pte Pritchett & NM 317 Pte Pratt rejoined from 76th D.H.Q. & NM 209 Pte A Sanderson Inspected by L.O.C 76th Division	

C. Hartley
Sgt Asst

Forwarded
Lieutenant Colonel Comd
1/1st N.M. Mobile Vety Section
1/5/16

Army Form C. 2118.

WAR DIARY
or
INTELLIGENCE SUMMARY.
(Erase heading not required.)

1/Lt N.M. Noble Vety Section

Instructions regarding War Diaries and Intelligence Summaries are contained in F. S. Regs., Part II. and the Staff Manual respectively. Title pages will be prepared in manuscript.

Place	Date	Hour	Summary of Events and Information	Remarks and references to Appendices
GRINCOURT	1/6/16		28 horses evacuated from LARBRET station. Capt HARTLEY resumes command	
"	3/6/16		of unit.	
			Q.M.S. TIBBS transferred from 4 LEICESTER REGT	
"	3/6/16		Inspection by D.D.V.S 3rd Army.	
"	2/6/16		36 horses evacuated.	
"	4/6/16		38 " "	
"	8/6/16		28 horses taken to LARBRET but returned to billet as the station had been	
"	10/6/16		shelled.	
"	11/6/16		25 horses evacuated from BOUQUEMASON.	
"	14/6/16		3 " " MONDICOURT	
"	15/6/16		3 " " LARBRET sent	
"			from 408. Div. Hd q 15	
"	21/6/16		34 horses evacuated from LARBRET.	
"	23/6/16		N.M. 50 Pte F.W. Fermor, N.M.140 Pte H.BULLINGTON promoted to	
"			rank of Paid acting Serjeant and attached to Artillery Bdes.	
"	24/6/16		24 sick evacuated from LARBRET. N.M.242 Pte J.Burgess	
"	28/6/16		24 " and 1 cast horse evacuated from LARBRET	

C Hartley Capt R.V.C

18 46

1/1 n.m. Mobile Vet Sec. Army Form C. 2118.

March

Vol. 3

WAR DIARY
or
INTELLIGENCE SUMMARY.
(Erase heading not required.)

Copy

Place	Date	Hour	Summary of Events and Information	Remarks and references to Appendices
	1/3/18		Evacuated 18 horses by road to 23 V.H. Two by motor ambulance	
	2/3/18		M.V.S. moved to Blainville les Aire	
	4/3/18		M.V.S. moved to Pottune	
	7/3/18		Evacuated 5 by barge	
	10/3/18		Evacuated 18 by barge	
	13/3/18		Evacuated 16 by barge	
	16/3/18		Evacuated 11 by barge	
	19/3/18		Evacuated 18 by barge	
	19/3/18		Evacuated 14 by barge	
	22/3/18		M.V.S. moved to Headingueul	
	23/3/18		Evacuated 23 by barge. M.V.S. moved to Bart.	
	25/3/18		Evacuated 15 by barge	
	29/3/18		Evacuated 13 by barge	
	31/3/18			

J. Wallace
Capt AVC T.F.

[Stamp: 1/1st (N.M.) MOBILE VETERINARY SECTION. 46th DIVISION.]

WAR DIARY
or
INTELLIGENCE SUMMARY.
(Erase heading not required.)

Army Form C. 2118.

Vol 14   1/1st N.M. Mobile Vety Section

Place	Date	Hour	Summary of Events and Information	Remarks and references to Appendices
ERMCOURT	1/2/17		Six men fitted with Box Respirators at the Gas School making the unit complete with the exception of Pte Brook who cannot be fitted at	
	4/2/17		Flight Recruit on leave to England	
	8/2/17		70 horses evacuated from MARINCOURT held up pro tem owing to traffic breakdown at AUTHIEULE CH.	
	15/2/17		31 animals evacuated from MARINCOURT CH	
	21/2/17		Capt T. Thomson A.V.C. takes over temporary command unit during absence of Capt Chartrey A.V.C. acting as A.D.V.S. Inspection of Sick Horses by A.D.V.S.	
	23/2/17		Evacuated 33- horses to 2.V.F.C. including 5-mange cases from MARINCOURT.	
	24/2/17		Remounts received by the division - total 96.	
	27/2/17		Corporal Russell returned from Leave	

T. Thomson
Capt A.V.C. (T)

WAR DIARY
or
INTELLIGENCE SUMMARY.
(Erase heading not required.)

Army Form C. 2118.

Instructions regarding War Diaries and Intelligence Summaries are contained in F. S. Regs., Part II. and the Staff Manual respectively. Title pages will be prepared in manuscript.

Vol XI
11th N.I.M. Mobile Vety Section

Place	Date	Hour	Summary of Events and Information	Remarks and references to Appendices
BECOURT	1/11/16		5 sick animals evacuated from BOUQUEMAISON STATION.	
BERGUIER	2/11/16		Marched to ST RIQUIER arriving at 3.30 p.m. No v/s from No 2 V. Hospital	
	3/11/16 to 21/11/16		All sick animals were evacuated to No 23 Vety Hospital, ABBEVILLE by road. Riding instruction etc was given to the unit on the training area and equipment overhauled and repaired.	
	22/11/16		Marched to MOULIN DE CRAMONT following H N.I.M.F.A. by R.E. and arrived at 1 p.m.	
	23/11/16		Marched to GOTREBOIS following 76th D.H.Q as far as WAVANS and arrived at 3.26 p.m.	
	25/11/16		Marched to LE MARAIS (FEC) DOULLENS arriving 10.45 a.m. Billeted at mill.	
	28/11/16		16 animals evacuated from DOULLENS	
	30/11/16		40 animals evacuated from Bocquemaison. From 28/11/16 the M.V.S. has been evacuating the horses of the 30th Div. R.F.A.	

C Hartley
Lt MRCVS

Army Form C. 2118.

Mob Vety Sec
VII 23

WAR DIARY
or
INTELLIGENCE SUMMARY.
(Erase heading not required.)

Instructions regarding War Diaries and Intelligence Summaries are contained in F. S. Regs., Part II. and the Staff Manual respectively. Title pages will be prepared in manuscript.

Place	Date	Hour	Summary of Events and Information	Remarks and references to Appendices
In field	3/11/17		Ten horses evacuated barge.	
	6/11/17		Seventeen horses evacuated barge.	
	13/11/17		Thirty seven horses evacuated barge. Inspection by D.V.S. on 9th inst.	
	15/11/17		Thirty five horses evacuated barge including eighteen from I Corps Veterinary Detachment	
			Received twenty five cases of sickness from I Corps V.D.	
	18/11/17		Thirty five horses evacuated barge	
	22/11/17		Forty horses evacuated barge	
	23/11/17		S/Sgt Gauntlett received from 12 V.H. Returned 14 days leave to England	
	24/11/17		Sgt Smith W.S. out to 12 V.H.	
	26/11/17		Pte Rich 14 days leave to England	
	27/11/17		Forty seven horses evacuated by two Thirty three by barge including eighteen from 37th MVS.	

John Tacet
Capt A.V.C. T.F.

1/1st (N.M.) MOBILE
VETERINARY SECTION,
46TH DIVISION.
No.
Date 30/11/17

WAR DIARY
or
INTELLIGENCE SUMMARY.
(Erase heading not required.)

Army Form C. 2118.

1/1st North Midland M.V.S.

WD 24

Place	Date	Hour	Summary of Events and Information	Remarks and references to Appendices
BETHUNE	1/12/17		Evacuated 68 horses by Barge	
"	4/12/17		Evacuated 40 Ophthalmia cases by train	
"	6/12/17		Evacuated 33 horses by Barge	
"	10/12/17		Evacuated 46 animals by Barge	
"	11/12/17		Evacuated 41 animals by train, including one with fatal S.E. 129 Sgt. CAMPLIN. S.E.; 2311 Pte STUBBS & 15886 Pte McKERNAN, from No 9 Vet. Hosp. were attached to this section to run the I CORPS, Horse Clipping Both.	
"	12/12/17		0379 Pte LITTLEWOOD proceeded on Leave U.K.	
"	13/12/17		10658 Pte. PRATT " " " " " " 5·4 animals evacuated by barge.	
"	14/12/17		Evacuate 25 animals by Barge.	
"	19/12/17		1.02439 Sgt. EDWARDS proceeded on 14 days leave.	
"	21/12/17		Going to bombing by enemy airmen 21 animals awaiting evacuation from 22 M.V.S. were killed by one bomb.	
"	23/12/17		Evacuated 27 animals by Barge including 1 cast by O.D.R. Another bombing raid took place but no damage done to the M.V.S.	
"	24/12/17		S.E. 1142 Sgt. WALTON proceeded on 14 days leave.	
"	26/12/17		CAPT. J. FACER proceeded on 14 days leave, CAPT. T. THOMSON taking over temp. command of M.V.S	
"	27/12/17		Evacuate 26 animals by barge.	
"	31/12/17		A bombing raid took place at 5·5·12M but no damage done to M.V.S. although 3 bombs dropped in the M.V.S. yard.	

G. Thomson
Capt. AVC (T.F.)
Capt. o.c. 1/1 (N.M.) M.V.S.

1/1/18.

Army Form C. 2118.

WAR DIARY
or
INTELLIGENCE SUMMARY.
(Erase heading not required.)

1/1st Mobile Vety Section

Place	Date	Hour	Summary of Events and Information	Remarks and references to Appendices
BARLIN	1/6/17		Evacuated 26 horses to 23 Vety. Hospital by train	
	2/6/17		Reinforcement received No. SE 2622 Pte. F. Traylor A.V.C.	
	3/6/17		No. T.T.02474 Pte. G. HOLLIS granted 10 days Leave to England.	
	4/6/17		No. T.T.02479 Pte. J. SIMPSON A.V.C. dispatched to No. 2 Vety. Hospital to replace	
	5/6/17		No. SE 2622 Pte. F. NAYLOR	
			Evacuated 6 horses by Barge to No. 23 Vety. Hospital, and 11 horses by train 2.23rd V.H.	
	8/6/17		Evacuated 6 horses by Barge and 6 horses by train to No. 23 Vety. Hospital.	
	11/6/17		Evacuated 6 horses by Barge including one horse cast by D.D.R. 1st Army	
			Capt. C. HARTLEY returned and took over charge of the M.V.S.	
	12/6/17		Evacuated 3 horses by train to No. 23 Vety. Hospital.	
			No. T. 34813 Sgt. J.A. DAY granted 10 days Leave to England.	
	14/6/17		Capt. C. Hartley proceeded on 10 days Leave to England + Capt. F. THOMSON	
			took over command of the M.V.S.	
			Reinforcement received No. 20037 Pte. H. BRADBURY	
	15/6/17		Evacuated 18 horses by train to No. 23 Vety. Hospital	

Army Form C. 2118.

46

WAR DIARY
or
INTELLIGENCE SUMMARY.
(Erase heading not required.)

Instructions regarding War Diaries and Intelligence
Summaries are contained in F. S. Regs., Part II.
and the Staff Manual respectively. Title pages
will be prepared in manuscript.

M.M.M.V.S
July 1915

Place	Date	Hour	Summary of Events and Information	Remarks and references to Appendices
In field	2/7/15		Staff Sergt Smell despatched to 3 G.H.B.	
	3/7/15		Evacuated 5 horses to V.&S.	
	6/7/15		Evacuated 5 horses to V.E.S.	
	8/7/15		Evacuated 8 " " "	
	13/7/15		" 4 " " "	
	14/7/15		" 9 " " "	
	13/7/15		" 12 " " "	
	14/7/15		" 5 " " "	
	15/7/15		" 8 " " "	
	19/7/15		Inspected by A.D.V.S. XIII Corps	
	22/7/15		Evacuated 9 horses to V.&S.	
	24/7/15		" 7 " " "	
	24/7/15		" 1 " " "	
	27/7/15		" 10 " " "	
	28/7/15		" 2 " " "	
	29/7/15		Pte Kennedy leave 6 days	
	31/7/15		" 9 " " "	

J. Rutoch
Capt M.O. T.F.

WAR DIARY
or
INTELLIGENCE SUMMARY.
(Erase heading not required.)

Army Form C. 2118.

1/1st H Mob Vety Sec

Place	Date	Hour	Summary of Events and Information	Remarks and references to Appendices
Infies	1/6/18		Evacuated nine horses to I Corps V.E.S.	
	3/6/18		Evacuated four horses to I Corps V.E.S.	
	5/6/18		Evacuated eight horses to I Corps V.E.S.	
	7/6/18		Evacuated ten horses to I Corps V.E.S.	
	8/6/18		Evacuated four horses to I Corps V.E.S.	
	10/6/18		Evacuated five horses to I Corps V.E.S.	
	12/6/18		Evacuated two horses to I Corps V.E.S.	
	13/6/18		Evacuated six horses to I Corps V.E.S.	
	15/6/18		Evacuated five horses to I Corps V.E.S.	
	19/6/18		Evacuated six horses to I Corps V.E.S.	
	23/6/18		Evacuated sixteen horses to I Corps V.E.S.	
	26/6/18		Evacuated eleven horses to I Corps V.E.S.	
	27/6/18		Evacuated eleven horses to I Corps V.E.S.	
	29/6/18		Evacuated three horses to I Corps V.E.S.	

WAR DIARY
or
INTELLIGENCE SUMMARY

Army Form C. 2118.

(Erase heading not required.)

Instructions regarding War Diaries and Intelligence Summaries are contained in F. S. Regs., Part II. and the Staff Manual respectively. Title pages will be prepared in manuscript.

Vol 8

Lieut N.M. Mobile Vety Station

Place	Date	Hour	Summary of Events and Information	Remarks and references to Appendices
SONCAMP FARM 035.a.2.6. Sheet 51C	1/8/16		21 animals evacuated to No 22 B.V.H. from LARBRET STATION	
	5/8/16		29 " " " " " " " "	
	8/8/16		NM 112 Pte Foster D. promoted to rank of Paid Acting Sergeant and attached to Section 46 AVDAC	
			NM 71 Pte Wells S.	O.B. 672 23rd Feb 1914
	19/8/16		24 animals evacuated to No 22 B.V.H. from LARBRET STATION	
	14/8/16		" " " " " " " " inspected by D.D.V.S.	
	15/8/16		23 animals evacuated to No 22 B.V.H. from LARBRET STATION	
	16/8/16		NM 299 Pte S.A. Brown & NM 320 Pte W.A. Brown from unit from England	
	17/8/16		16 animals evacuated to No 22 B.V.H. from LARBRET Station.	
	20/8/16		2 animals " " " " " "	
	23/8/16		29 " " " " " " "	
	25/8/16	9.4 am	The M.V.S. moved to the farm of M Villerval at LARBRET at which place there had been an Advanced Post.	
	28/8/16		3 horses evacuated to No 22 B.V.H. from LARBRET Station	

C Huntley
Capt AVC

Army Form C. 2118.

WAR DIARY
or
INTELLIGENCE SUMMARY.
(Erase heading not required.)

Unit N.M. Mob Vety Section

Instructions regarding War Diaries and Intelligence Summaries are contained in F. S. Regs., Part II. and the Staff Manual respectively. Title pages will be prepared in manuscript.

Place	Date	Hour	Summary of Events and Information	Remarks and references to Appendices
ROELLECOURT	1/5/16		N.M. 64 Pte Sampson reports unit.	
"	2/5/16		39 horses evacuated from St Pol	
"	5/5/16		29 horses " " 2 remount cases from St Pol	
"	6/5/16	1.30am	Fire breaks out in billet	
"	7/5/16		13 horses evacuated from St Pol	
"	8/5/16		Move to GRINCOURT	
"	9/5/16		Capt Hartley resumes command of unit	
GRINCOURT	10/5/16		36 horses evacuated from LARBRET	
"	14/5/16		N.M. 106 Pte B Ford, N.M. 124 Pte W Bennoy N.M. 4 Cpl H S. promoted to rank of	
"	15/5/16		L/cpl acting Sergeants and attached to Artillery Brigade	
"	17/5/16		Capt Hartley & 7 men innoculated with Horse Typhoid Vaccine	
"	18/5/16		39 horses evacuated	
"	19/5/16		N.M. Pte Burgess & N.M. Pte Palmer join unit from England	
"			N.M. Pte Abbot transferred to 7th Div Hdqts.	
"	21/5/16		23 sick horses and 1 remount case evacuated	
"	22/5/16		Capt. Facer A.V.C. F.R. takes over temp command of unit.	
"	25/5/16		25 horses evacuated	
"	28/5/16		28 horses "	

C. Hartley Capt AVC T

WAR DIARY
or
INTELLIGENCE SUMMARY
(Erase heading not required.)

Army Form C. 2118.

Place	Date	Hour	Summary of Events and Information	Remarks and references to Appendices
	28/7/17 26/7/17		Evacuated 9 horses by barge & 8 mange by train. Copied Russell T.T 62490 evacuated.	

John Facer.
Capt. A.V.C. (T.F.)

Date.	Place.	Summary of information.

Lieut. N.M. Mosley-Leaton

Feb 1. 1916.   Lieut N M Mobile Kelly Leaton billeted at Maizens
sous-AILLY CH.

Feb 12. 1916.   Corpl M Sulliot promoted to rank of Sergeant (paid) and
attached to 139 x Inf Bgde CH.
Cpl A M Carty promoted to rank of Corporal CH
During the foregoing period such arrivals were evacuated
by road to No 22 B.V.H, and the motor ambulance belonging
to that Hospital were found unsuitable for the work
regions cases CH.

Feb 10 1916   Marched to RIBEAUCOURT CH
Feb 28 1916   Marched to FIENVILLERS CH

C Hartley Capt. R.A.M.C.T.
O.C. N.M. Mobile Kelly Section

WO 95/26814

1/ N.M.
1/1st Nor. Mid. Fd. Amb. (46th Div)
March 1915 – Dec 1916
Vol I

To
D.A.D.V.S
46th DIVSN.

I regret clerical error in War Diary. D.V.S. I ARMY visited this section on 9/11/17. Amended & returned please

Johnson(?)
Capt a.v.c
17

1/1st (N.M.) MOBILE
VETERINARY SECTION,
46th DIVISION.
No............
Date 4-12-17

46

1/1 N.M. Mob Vety Sec
Vol III

.46

1/1 NM Mob Vety Sec
―――――――
Vol II

www.ingramcontent.com/pod-product-compliance
Lightning Source LLC
Chambersburg PA
CBHW081242170426
43191CB00034B/2014